The Adventures of Big Head Bob

By David Bradley

The Adventure Of Big Head Bob. All rights reserved.
Copyright 2020 © David Bradley

No part of this book may be reproduced in any form or by any electronic or mechanical means, including information storage and retrieval systems, without the permission in writing from the author. However, reviewers may quote brief passages in a review. Please contact the author here info@BigHeadBob.com.

Based on a true story...

Big Head Bob was
crying in his bed.

Sobbing to his mother
about his big Bob head.

"People treat me
like an unwanted toy.

I wish I could just
be a normal boy!"

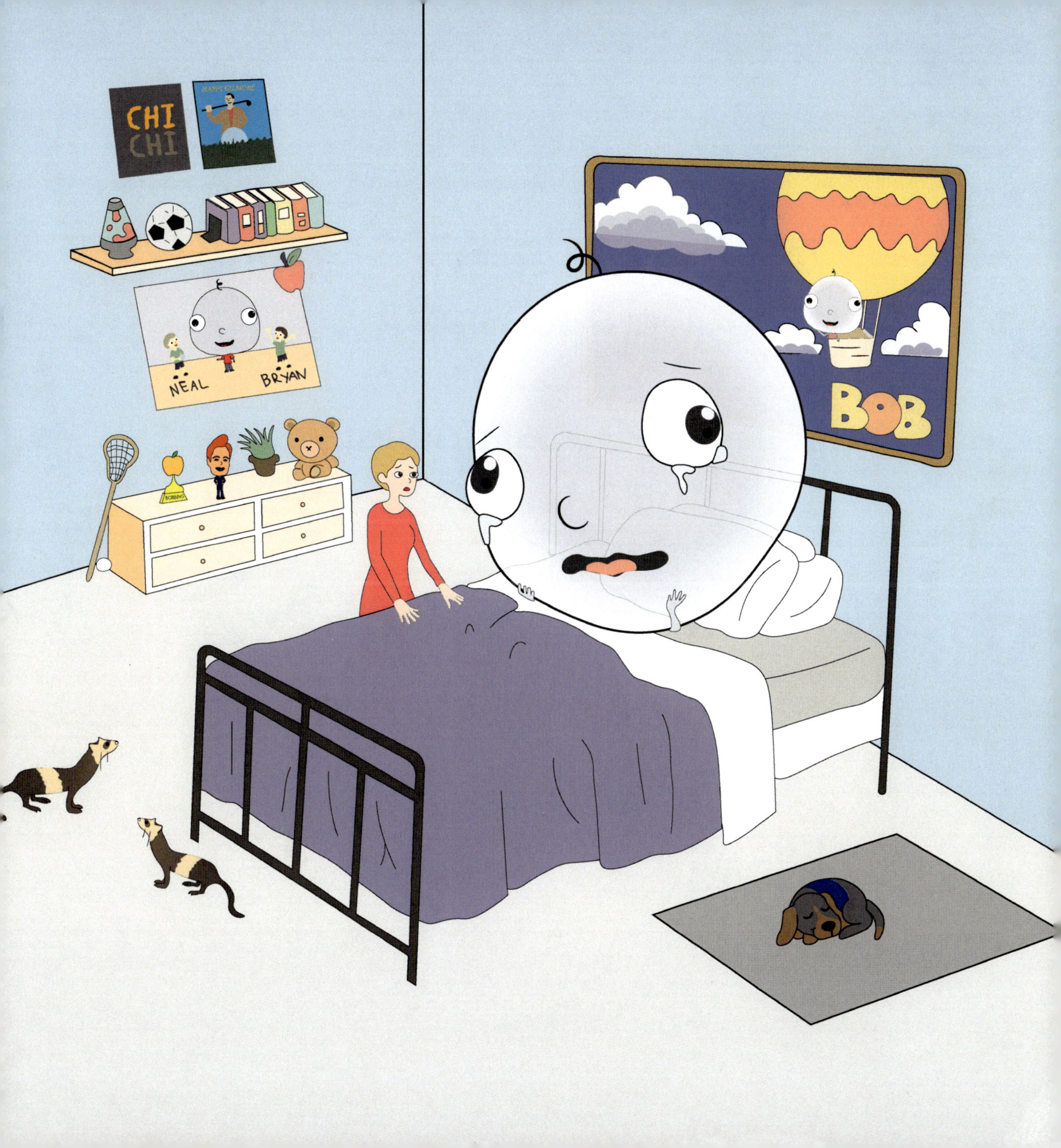
CHI CHI
HAPPY GILMORE
NEAL
BRYAN
BOB

Big Head Bob was feeling quite sad and moody.

So Bob took his big head to see a movie.

Once seated, the crowd turned angry and red.

"HEY, Bob! We can't see past your big round head!"

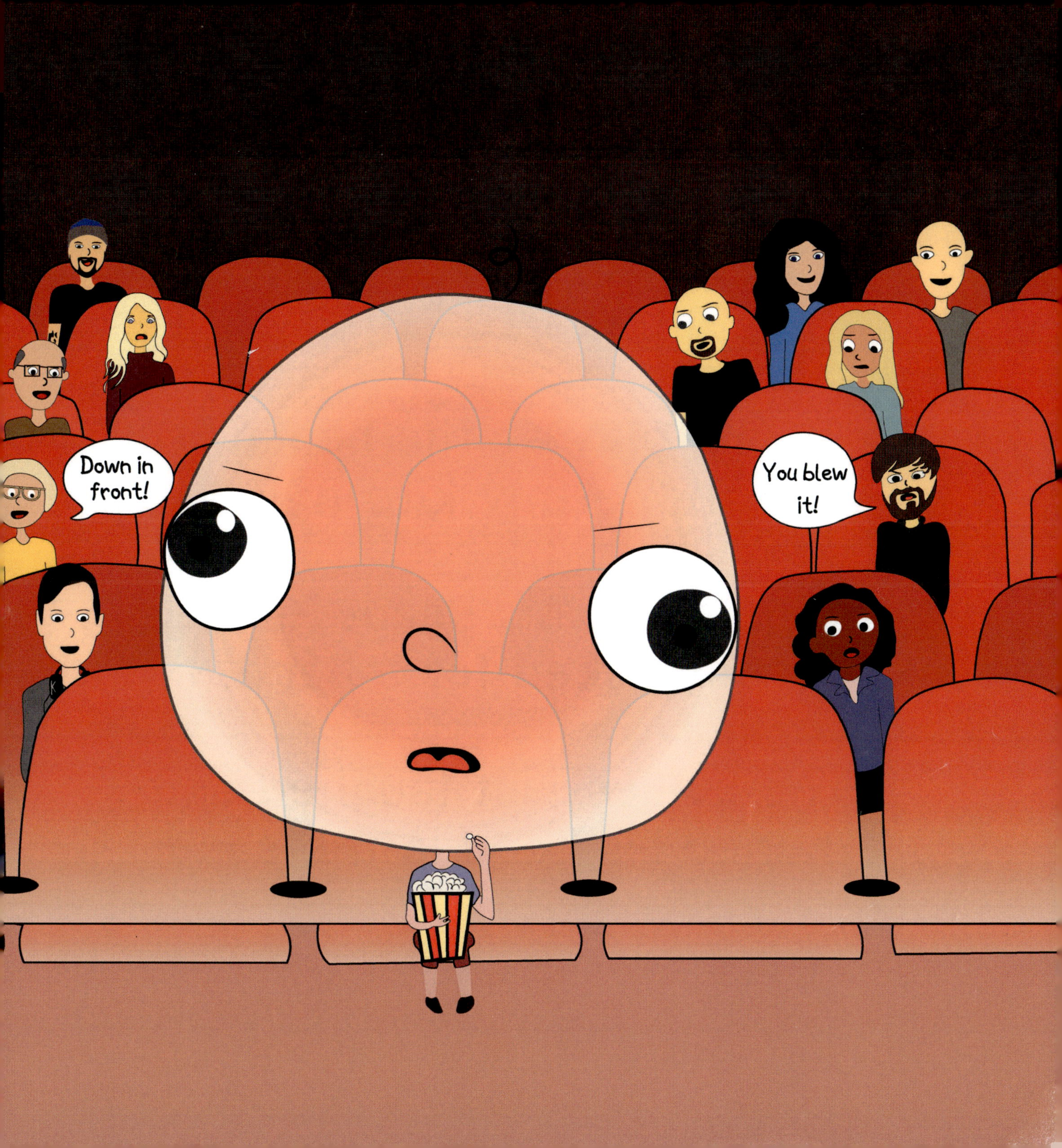
Down in front!
You blew it!

"Oh boy, I'm so sad,"
Bob started to cry.

"I'll play at the beach
and let my kite fly!"

While flying his beautiful kite,
Bob asked for a hand.

The bullies just laughed and
buried his head in the sand!

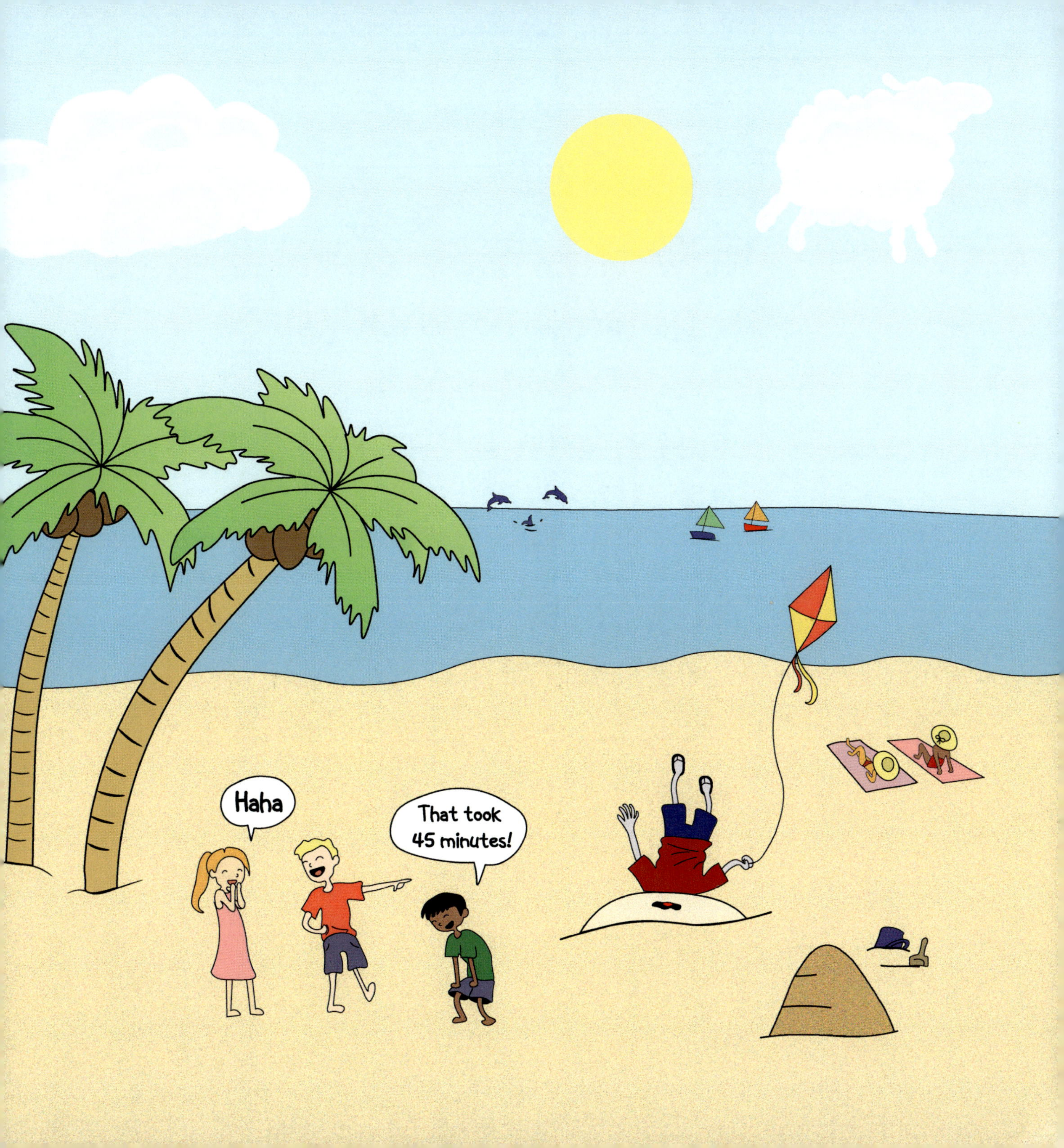
Haha
That took 45 minutes!

Now this may come
as quite the shocker,

Big Head Bob was
no good at soccer.

In sports, he wasn't
welcome to play.

"Move Bob, your big
HEAD is in the way!"

"Baba Booey!"

"Oh boy..."

Big Head Bob craved
adventure to feel alive.

"I will swim with the
fishes and SCUBA dive."

Bob screamed as he fell
in the water far from shore.

Bob's big head, like an anchor,
sank to the sea floor.

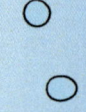

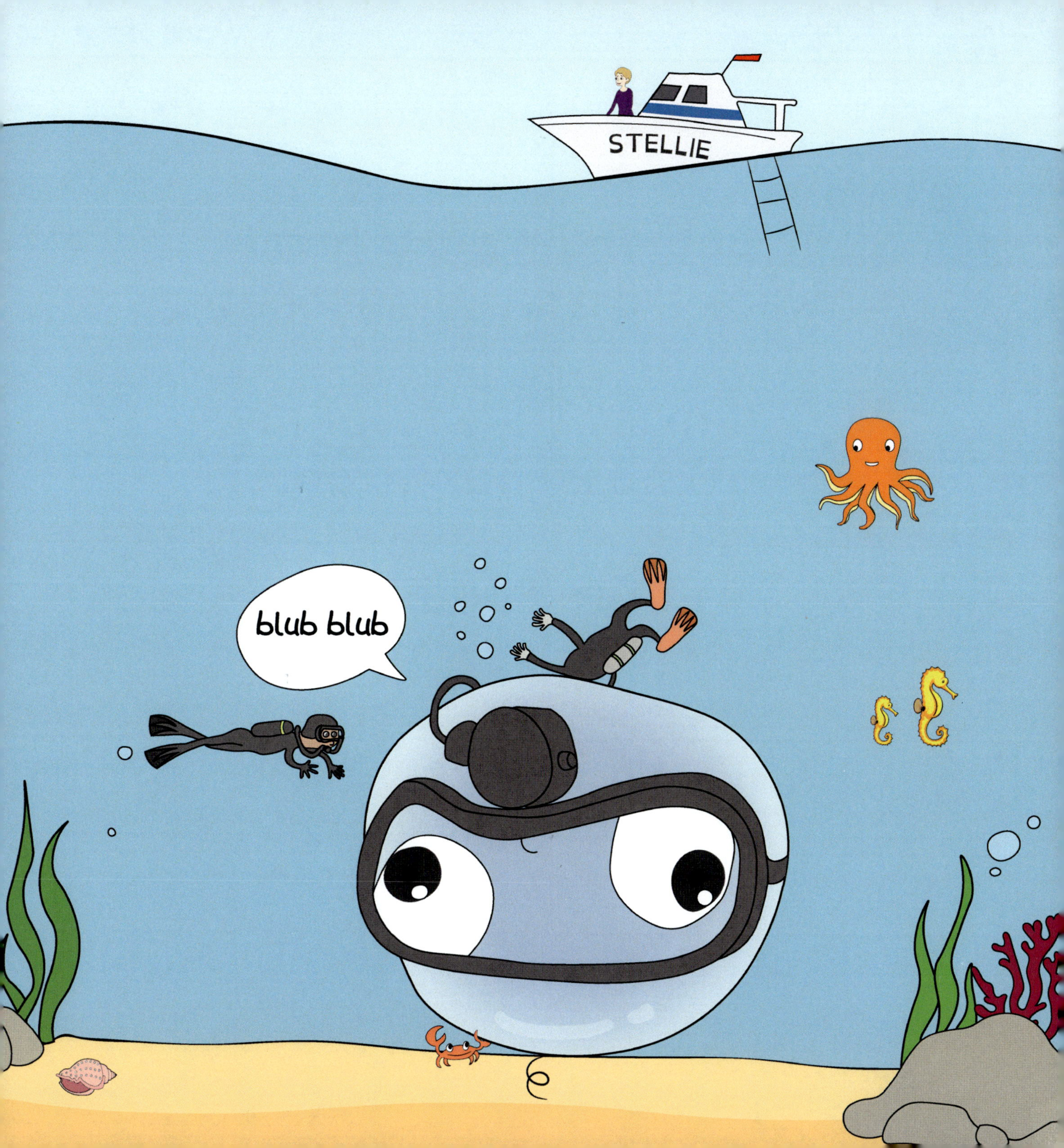
STELLIE
blub blub

Bob and his big head
were frustrated at length.

"I must transform my
weakness into strength.

I'm tired and done
with this aggravation.

It's time I evolve and
learn meditation."

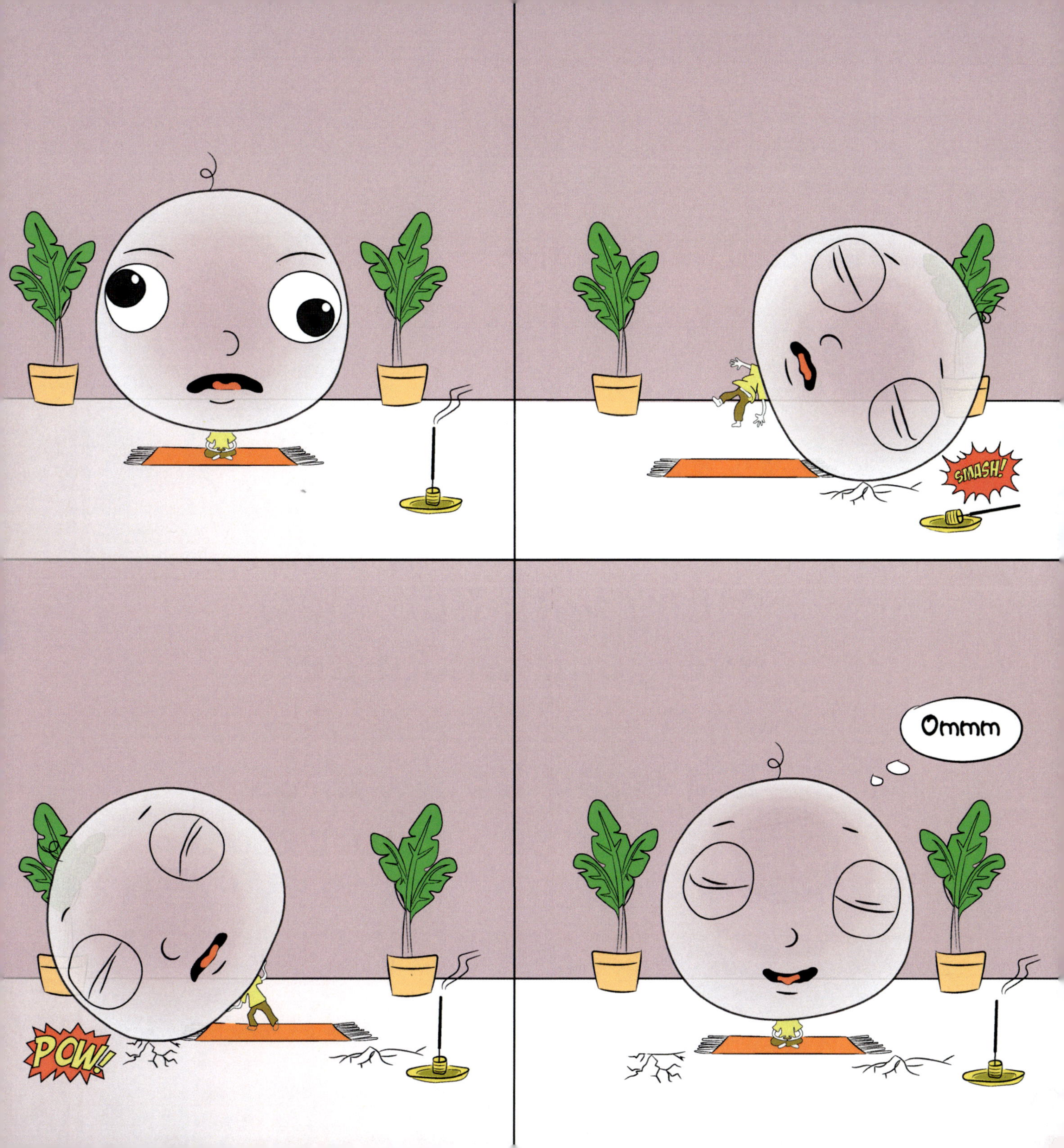
SMASH!
POW!
Ommm

Bob thought it was best to sit in the back.

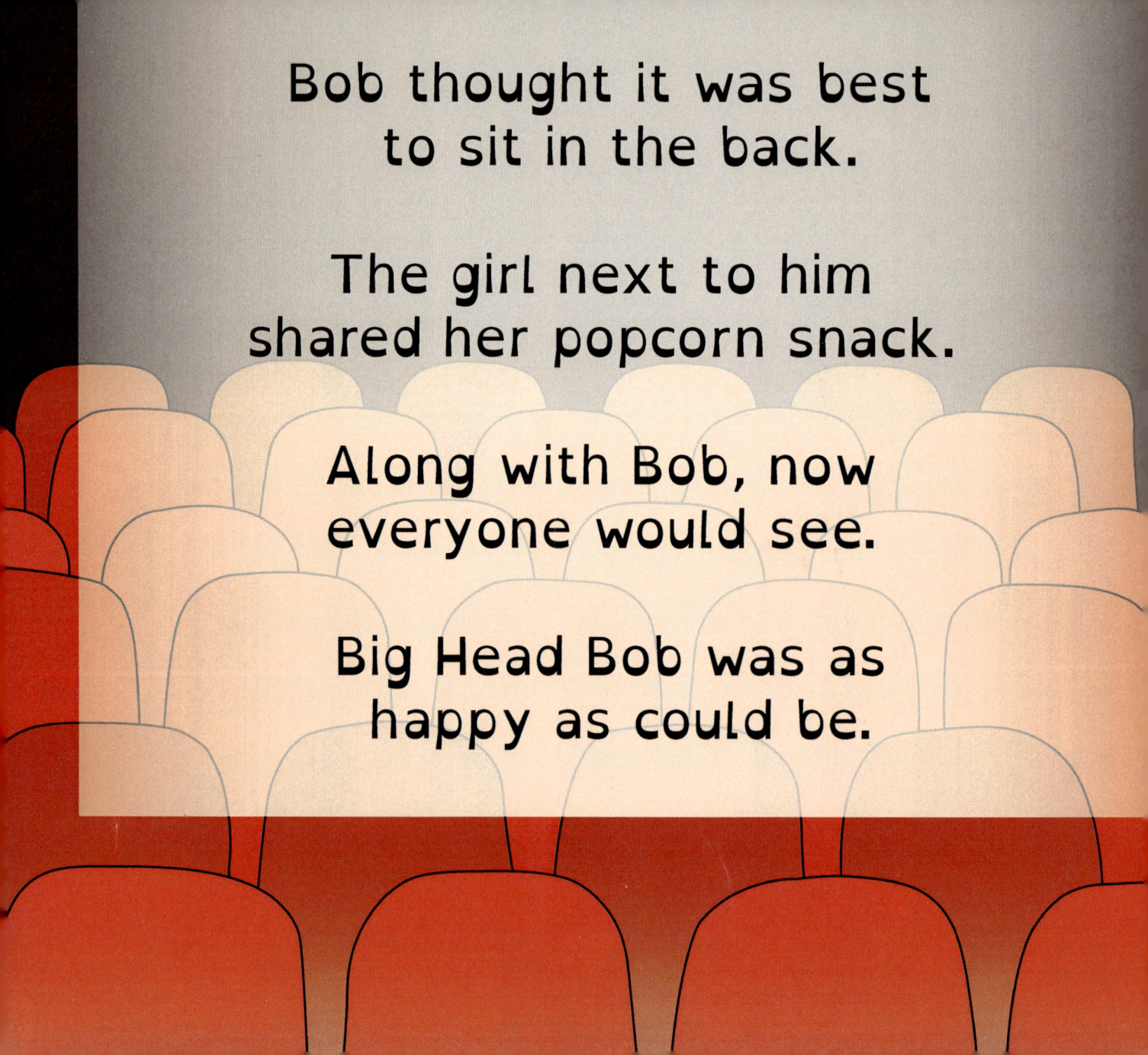

The girl next to him shared her popcorn snack.

Along with Bob, now everyone would see.

Big Head Bob was as happy as could be.

"Yeth"

"Would you like to join me?"

Tied in overtime, the coach
put Bob into the game.

With a match-winning goal,
all would cheer Bob's name.

By thinking clearly, he knew
to stand near the net.

The ball bounced off his
head and a score he would get!

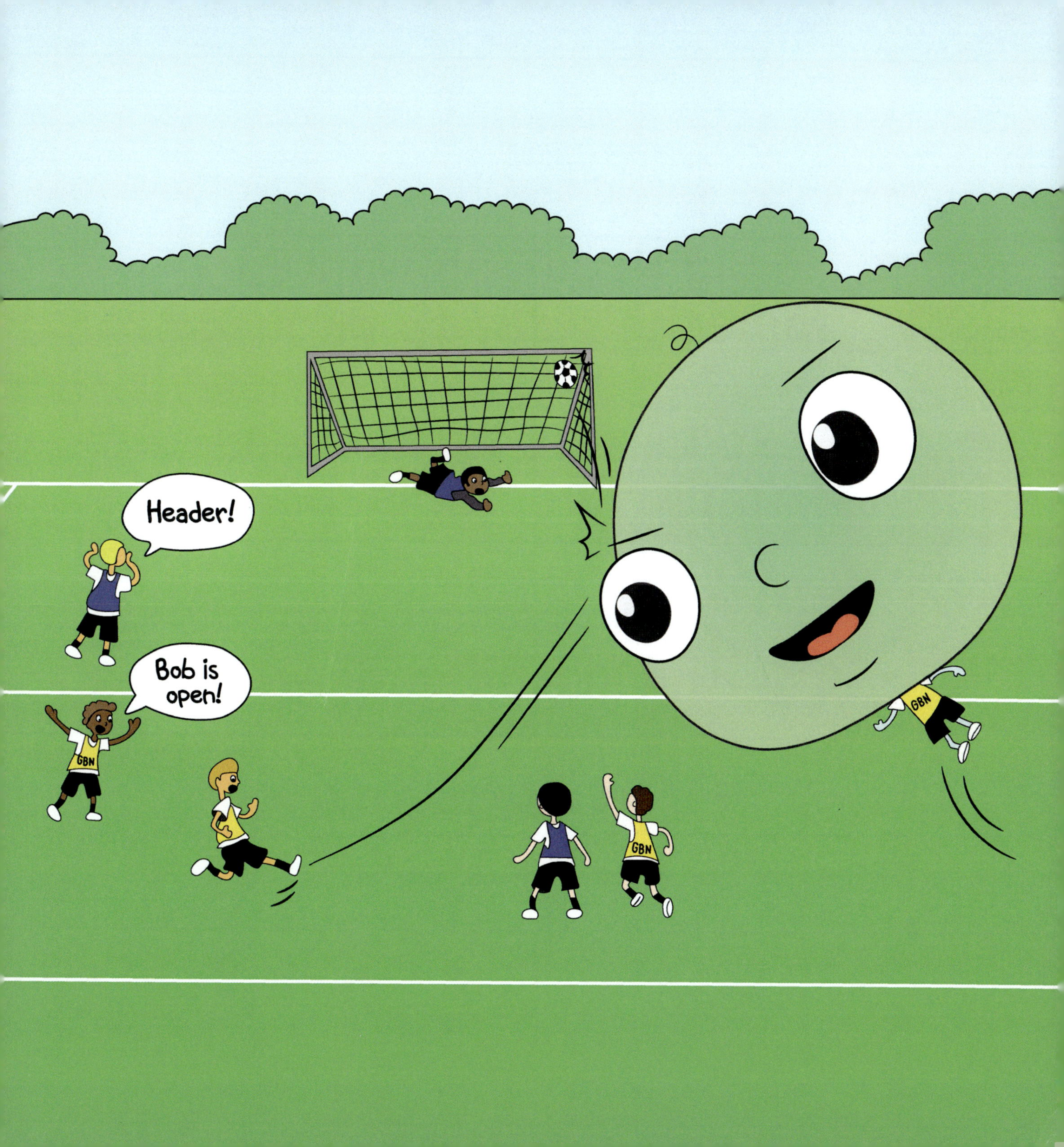
Header!
Bob is open!

Big Head Bob wanted someone's day to be made.

So he offered his head to provide some shade.

"Wow Bob, you are so thoughtful and sweet!

Will you be my friend and come have a seat?"

"Life is a roller coaster
with ups and downs.

Always try your best with
smiles and not frowns.

'Stay positive and breathe'
is what we now say.

Just WOW! That was one
heck of a cawwwazy day!"

"What a CWAZY day!"

Lessons & Vocabulary
The more you know

SOBBING is when you cry...a lot. Tears come down your face and that is okay. You are feeling emotions. When you finish crying, you are stronger!

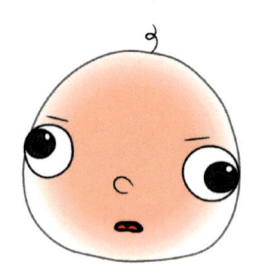

When feeling **MOODY** it's important to realize that it is normal. These emotions are temporary, take a deep breath and talk to someone around you. Don't worry, you are not alone.

BULLIES are people that feel bad and want you to feel bad too. Understanding their point of view will help you stay happy because that is your goal. Be strong and ask for help when dealing with a bully.

SHOCKER is when you are super surprised! Some people like it, some people don't.

People shout **BABA BOOEY** when someone makes a fool of themselves or as a distraction.

An **ANCHOR** is a heavy metal object used to steady a boat in the water. Some people are referred to as an anchor.

SCUBA Stands for Self Contained Underwater Breathing Apparatus. With proper training, you can breathe with an air tank underwater and see a whole new world.

Bob was **AGGRAVATED** and **FRUSTRATED**. Try to understand what bothers you and then work on a way to be happier. Calm yourself down, relax and try again.

Be like Bob and **TRANSFORM** negative feelings into positive ones. You just need to use your head, whatever size it may be.

EVOLVE is when you grow and change just like a butterfly. There may be pain in growing but it can lead to great change if you stay patient.

MEDITATION is a practice of calming your thoughts and mind. Clearing your mind can help you recharge for any situation.

STRENGTH is power. Power your mind, body, and soul.

WEAKNESS is when you are not at your best. You can become stronger by practicing patience and creativity daily.

SHARING is offering what you have to another person. An easy way to remember why we do this are the words, "sharing is caring." We must care for each other.

BEING AWARE of your surroundings affects others and can make a big impact. By moving his seat in the theater, Bob's head was out of the way and that helped everyone, including himself.

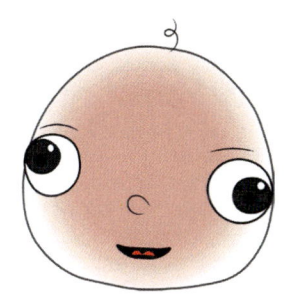

By **THINKING CLEARLY**, Bob moved closer to the goal and that gave the team a better chance of winning! In life, the slightest change can make the biggest difference.

Bob's head is so big...HOW BIG IS IT? When the sun shined bright, his head acted as an umbrella, providing some cool shade. It's possible that the cause of a problem could also be the solution. Use your **IMAGINATION**.

CWAZY is Crazy, tee HEE hee.

Acknowledgements

Baby Joaqun, you are the inspiration for this book. When I told you this fact at 3 months old you quickly responded by spitting up all over my shirt. It's all good baby! You are an inspiration to our family and we will make you proud.

The first page is an actual memory of my mother when I was a boy. Occasionally, I would miss gym class due to tutoring classes. On those school nights, I would cry to my mom and say, "I wish I was just a normal boy." She has reminded me of this story constantly over the past 20 years and adds, "Look at you now." I love you, mom.

To my brothers Neal, Bryan, and Gabe. Together we have been able to identify our weaknesses and help each other transform them one by one into strengths. I love you and I would not be me, without you.

To my cousins, I dedicate this art to you in hopes that it brings inspiration. You are intelligent, kind, and a brilliant reflection of your parents. Asher, Eden, Ella and Ruby, Eli and Zachary, Gabe, Judah and Noah. Adina, Eliana, Roie and Yoni.

To the children...Ivy, Chloe, Lilah and Sadie, Crosby and Jude, Dash, Isaac, Jaxon, Lee and Micah, Ace and Alec, Violet, Maxwell, Benny and Ava, Aria and Toby, Chase and Parker, Rocky and Alaia, Leni, Jayden, Ryder and Penelope, Rena, Giuliana, Roman, Liam, and Olivia.

Thank you Param Srivastava for creating brilliant illustrations with me. This art is bringing joy to all.

Finally, I'd like to thank you. Yes, YOU! As Grandma Ethel use to say, "Wishing you health, happiness and all that life has to offer."

Follow Me...

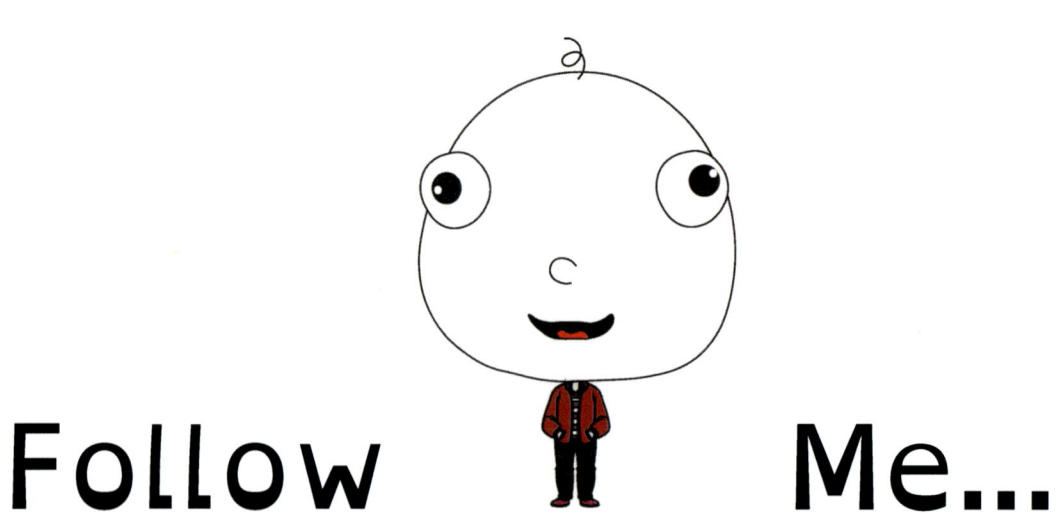

@BigHeadBob

/iambigheadbob

www.BigHeadBob.com

BigHeadBob

Made in the USA
Monee, IL
23 February 2021